Cracking all drug addiction

OTENG MONTSHITI

Cracking alcoholism and drug addiction
Copyright ©2019
CONTACT ADDRESS: OTENG MONTSHITI
P O BOX M1139
KANYE
BOTSWANA

E-MAIL ADDRESS: otengmontshiti@gmail.com
Contact number: (+267) 74 644 954

Table of contents

Part A

Acknowledgements-4

Chapter 1

Childhood-5

Chapter 2

Growth-14

Chapter 3

Maturity- 20

Chapter 4

The turning point-28

Chapter 5

Lessons 1 have learned in life-36

Chapter 6

Parental guidance is important-40

Chapter 7

Don't blame other people-45

Chapter 8

Never give up-50

Part B

Chapter 1

Secrets of maintaining a free alcohol and drug addiction life-54

Chapter 2

Steps of breaking alcohol and drug addiction-63

Acknowledgements

Writing a book is not an easy task. Therefore I would like to thank our lord Jesus Christ, my family especially my lovely wife who supported.

Part A

Cracking alcoholism and drug addiction

childhood

Kanye is one of the major villages in Botswana. It is almost ninety seven kilometers from the capital city of Botswana known as Gaborone.

It is in the southern hemisphere. It is a wonderful place,

surrounded by magnificent hills covered with beautiful tress, cascading colorful flowers and rolling stones.

This is where 1 was brought up by a single parent (my lovely mother). When 1 was born or grew up it was not well developed. It was just a small typical African village. 1 loved to play mud village and football in the dusty street of Kanye when I was a small kid. According to my mother my father abandoned us when I was born on the 28 September 1979. The reason is only known by her. I am the last born of eight children (six brothers and two sisters). All my brothers have passed away but my sisters are still alive.

I remember my

mother told me that one of my family members kicked her out in the middle of the night and she walked into the darkness of the town of Lobatse. She found and slept in a toilet for three continuous days. To make matters worse when she went to work she would put my food on top of a toilet seat.

My family was

extremely poor when I grew up. We used to live in an uncompleted house. That is to say our traditional mud house had no wall. We lived in house covered with tree branches acting as a wall. To make matters worst half of the house was roofed the other part was uncovered.

During raining seasons it was not a pretty sight at all. We would all move to the covered side. In the morning our wet blankets, clothes, mattresses and other materials could be seen moving to and fro on the washing line.

I was known as stubborn child in my community. My neighbors would beat the hell out of me. They did that out of ignorance. Many

people thought I was
stubborn while in
actual fact there was
an empty space in my
heart. I needed fatherly
love but no one was
available.

I grew up like that with
that empty space or
monster eating me
inside but no one
knew what I was
going through. I just
needed some to act as
a fatherly figure. We
were asked by elderly

people in the community to help them to prepare traditional beer and we were rewarded with a cup of it. They thought it was healing something in the stomach while in actual fact they were introducing us into the world of alcoholism. That's why ignorance is every dangerous.

Many years went by but the struggle

continued. To put the food on the table my mother worked as farm laborer during harvesting seasons. She was paid with bags of beans, maize and sorghum to sustain the family. She was a mother, father and husband at the same time.

Chapter 2

Growth

I grew up like that until I was sent to a primary school closer to my home. The same problem of stubbornness followed me there. I was labelled as a stubborn child by teachers. No one cared to investigate my background.

Most of the time

teachers would slap me in front of other students to humiliate me. Then, 1 would leave the classroom went come and come with my mother. She would come to my rescue. Still none of my teachers asked the root cause of my problem.

1 passed primary and went to junior secondary the bad behavior was still part of my being.

No matter how much I tried the situation persisted.

While I was doing my first year at junior school I was introduced into drinking by other students. During the weekends we would drink a lot. I did all this behind my mothers back. When she thought I was asleep I would jump over the window. and went to the bars.

I completed my secondary school education in 2000. I started to drink excessively almost every day. When I got some money I would spend the whole night drinking alcohol. Sometimes we would fight one another until the police intervened.

At home it was a disaster my siblings started to hate my character.

They stopped helping me. I was all alone in the dark world of my own with no one in particular to comfort me.

The only person who had faith in me was my mother. She would give me money or bought me clothes behind their back. I was a total shame to my family. I was tortured inside.

I went to technical college to do information technology but the habit followed me there. But I managed to complete the programme by special grace of God.

Chapter 3

Maturity

I wanted to work in the army but I was not successful. Then I applied to a very powerful organization and I was very successful.

I went home almost every weekend and I would drink like it was my last day on earth. When Monday came I wouldn't be available at work. I would be penniless. My mother would go around and borrowed money from our neighbors. Then, I would return to work the following day in the morning.

As time went by I would be absent from work for two continuous days. Warning letters were written but I turned a deaf ear to those warning letters.

The behavior of alcoholism went on and on until my employer was left with no alternative but to sack me. The reality started to sink in my head but it was too late. The destruction had been done beyond correction.

I was tortured by bad thoughts everyday. That is to say suicidal thoughts started to brew but I feared death.

I thought of committing an offence and went to prison but the fear of prison stopped me.

I took all my benefits and spent it in alcohol. Then I started stealing money from home to finance my drinking problems. I would tell them that I had been invited for an interview while in actual fact I was a liar. Because of that they rejected me even the more.

I started chopping fire woods for neighbors to generate funds for my drinking habits. Some of them would take me to their lands to work as farmer labor. Just image a graduate of information technology doing those things.

I thought that was how my life was programmed to be.

I accepted my failure
i.e. I was totally
helpless. I couldn't
handle any job at that
time and my friends
abandoned me.

Then I started to
become sick on regular
basis and the root
cause was alcoholism.
I started to sweat
profusely and pain
was all over my body.
Doctors and nurses
told me to stop
drinking alcohol

but I failed on number of occasions until I gave up.

I went to various clinics to seek professional counseling but all in vain. I would stop for few days then the urge would overcome me and I would start drinking again.

I couldn't maintain any relationship. Every

relationship 1 entered into was a disaster because 1 had another relationship with alcoholism. My destructive relationship with alcohol would destroy everything. Then 1 would be left all alone.

Chapter 4

The turning point
(John 3:16)

2012 was a wonderful year in my life. I was invited by a friend of mine to a local church. The church was full that day. It was a wonderful evening and wonderful breeze was blowing across the village of Kanye. The stars were shining bright in the sky.

We were taught the word of God (sermon) and then we were prayed for. From that wonderful night up to today I have never tasted alcohol. I am totally free from alcohol addiction.

I started worshipping with them. The urge to drink disappeared completely. I was totally restored.

Within the gap of

three months I was
employed by one of
the powerful company
in Botswana. I worked
for four months then
resigned because my
sponsorship had been
approved. The best part
of it was that I had a
wonderful relationship
with my bosses. I was
rarely absent from
work, obedient and
very punctual.

My family members
were very skeptical at
first

but as time went by they started to realize that I had changed completely and started to trust me. I was no longer a trouble maker. The character of lying stopped and fighting habit dropped.

I completed my marketing programme in 2015. I was given an award of "best student in marketing management 2014/2015".

I was very unique at school. I maintained an attendance record of ninety nine percent. I did assignments without teachers instructing me because I knew my future was in my hands.

I remember one day students wanted to strike, I told them in their eyes that I am not part of that strike. I was there to build my future and my future was not in the hands of teachers but in the hands of God. They were shocked.

Another incident was when they refused to write examinations and they blamed teachers. I raised my hands and said, "The question that we should ask ourselves is, is Institute of Commercial Management (ICM) student or lecture centered?"

We agreed it is student centered. Everyone was shocked.

One of our lecturers told me that, "1 have taught for over eighteen years but i have never heard any student speaking like that. That wisdom is not from you it is from above."

At the end of the same year 1 married my wife, a

wonderful, beautiful
woman and full of
wisdom. Today we are
happily married and
we have our own
house. Life is
wonderful. The lord
has blessed me
mightily in all the
areas of my life.

Chapter 5

Lessons 1 have learned in life

Spiritual and physical
Spiritual (Genesis 1)

Spiritual controls the physical world. It is where God resides and manufacture things. Some of the problems we are facing as human beings the root cause is spiritual (spiritual problems). Problems that you have no power to overcome in this world are spiritual.

The spiritual addresses the spiritual. If you are drinking or engaged in drugs and you can't refrain from that on your own you need spiritual intervention. In simple words you need to be prayed for and break those chains. God takes care of our spiritual needs.

Physical

Professionals like nurses, doctors take care of physical needs like good health. They treat the flesh but God heals. They need Godly strength and wisdom to do their jobs. In my case they did not fail my problem was spiritual.

Anything that you are fighting for and you fail to overcome it using earthly methods like healing, counseling etc. it is simply spiritual. Therefore you need God to address your situation.

Chapter 6

<u>Parental guidance is important</u> Parents should train their children in the rightful (Godly way) so that when they are fully grown up they may not depart from the truth. As a parent you should know your children deeply. That is to say you should know what they are doing, the kind of friends they keep etc.

because the world is not a safe place to be. Children are under constant attack from various sources like teenage pregnancy, alcohol and drug addiction, and other criminal activities.

Parents must make sure that their children are in their rooms before going to bed. They should check up on them on regular basis during the course of the night. Because some of them jump over the window like I used to do.

In simple words they should be their friends. They should share life issues with them because that is how they can be empowered. Life without knowledge is very destructive.

Ignorance is destruction in disguise. You should teach them never trust or follow any stranger because human trafficking is on the rise. It is not only that children kidnapping is also on the rise.

Teach them to focus on their education because it the key to a better world. Life without education is life without meaning and purpose.

It also leads to poor decision making and poor decision making leads to a weak world.

Chapter 7

Don't blame other people

One thing that 1 have learned in life is that you won't grow up if you blame innocent people. Your development will be delayed. We should be responsible for own actions.

If you fail at school don't blame teachers but

blame yourself.
Teachers are just
catalysts of life. They
help you to discover
your potential but to
do your purpose it is
your portion. Above all
you can reject
whatever they tell you.
It is like someone who
gives you a gift; you
can accept it or reject
it. In this world
everyone was born
free and no one can
force you to receive
something you don't

want unless you
permit him or her.

Today I don't blame
anybody about what
happened to me but I
have learned life the
hard way so that I
may give my children a
better life. I have
learned to share my
experience with others
so that the future of
this world can be
secured. I truly believe
that whatever I went
through in life Godly

purpose was behind it.

Teachers on the other hand should not just harass students without knowing the root cause of their problem. They should make thorough investigation so that they can come up excellent ways of helping them instead of labelling them with funny names.

They should act as fathers to the fatherless, mothers to the motherless, comfort those who are in pain, heal the broken hearted. Teachers are agents of change. They should partner with parents to reshape the future of their children.

Chapter 8

Never give up
(Jeremiah 18)

Instead of blaming innocent people you should know that everything that happens under the sun Godly purpose is behind it. If you are poor there is Godly purpose behind your situation. It might be to teach you the pain of lacking so that when you are successful you

may bless other
people.

Bad habits like
alcoholism and drugs
are not part of your
future. They are
destructive elements.
Don't embrace them
fight them.

Don't be a degenerated
criminal or drug addict
because broken things
are useful in the hands
of God.

If you surrender your problem unto him he will restore you to your original condition, like he did to me in 2012.

If you read bible from Genesis to Revelations God changed wicked people and stated to use them to change the world. We make the world a better place if we share ideas and experiences because people will

learn from our
mistakes. Iron
sharpens an iron. For
example you should
tell other people about
the dangerous part of
drug addiction.

Part B

Chapter 1

Secrets of maintaining a free alcohol and drug addiction life.

1. The word of God
The word of god is the final gift of love from God. The more you read it the more you are empowered. It re programs your mind so that it can be aligned with the promises of God.

Our character is formed by what we read. If you read destructive materials it is not healthy. Your mind will start to think along that line and what you read has great influence in your behavior. If someone is violent the root cause is wrong mentality.

If you read the word of God without meditation it won't change your behavior.

If you read it meditatively it will change you. Your negative thoughts will be transformed into positive thoughts.

Since 2012, I fill my mind with positive thoughts no matter what I am going through. I view life differently. When I am going through financial dryness I know it is temporary. That is the power of the mind, it has the power to destroy or build you.

1. Testimony

Don't sit down and keep quite share your ideas, experience with other people. The world is in deep trouble it needs what you have to be a better place. You should give other people hope, those who are discouraged encourage them and so forth. Share with other people what you have or know using every channel that is available like twitter, face book, word of mouth etc.

If you speak out you are healing or liberating yourself. You will feel relieved. Above all you will save someone's life who is about to do something funny like committing suicide, committing abortion etc.

3. Keeping the right friends
(Psalm 1: 1-7)

There are two types of friends in this world namely; those who are in your outer circle and those who are in your inner circle. Friends who are in your inner cycle should be people who believe in your abilities, focused in life, don't support your weaknesses and challenge your creativity.

While those who are in **NOTES** your outer circle should be people who doubt your potential. Lack focus in life, pull you down, never give you new ideas and supports your weakness like short temper, jealousy etc. In life if you don't have direction you cant direct anybody. Don't hate them but love them at a distance.

Today 1 only keep people

who motivate me to work hard in life but before 1 used to keep wrong friends in my inner cycle.

Prayer (Luke 18:1)

Prayer is part our walk with the lord.it is an investment in eternity. Christianity without prayer is incomplete. It is when you communicate with God or the invisible world and receive answers from him. It is not a

monologue it is a
dialogue.

It edifies your spirit. It
makes your sprit light
and be attractive to God.
It aligns your spirit with
the spirit of God.

Prayer has helped me to
maintain my freedom. I
pray without easing
because I know I need
his strength everyday. I
strongly recommend it
to everyone.

Chapter 2
Steps of breaking alcohol and drugs addiction

1. <u>Accept that you have a problem</u>

The first thing in problem solving is to accept that you have a problem. If you don't accept that you have a problem then the solution is just a distant memory. You are the most important person in the equation.

If people counsel you but you don't accept that you have a problem(s) there is totally nothing that can be done to help you to get out of your mess. There is one simple rule in this world there is nothing that can be done in your life without your approval. Where there is an acceptance there is willingness to change.

If you have accepted that

you have a problem(s)
you are step closer to
your solution.

2. Willingness to change
 (Psalm 37: 4) The next
thing in life is your
willingness to change.
As 1 said earlier there is
nothing that can be
done against your will.
Even God can't give you
what you don't want. He
makes suggestions but
the final decision is in
your

hands. For example, you can reject his suggestions it is still fine with him because he will never override your will.

Professionals like nurses, doctors etc. can advice you but if you are not ready to change there is nothing that can be done. That is to say, they can advice, correct or encourage you but the final decision is in hands. Every man has been given the power to decide his future.

Servants of God can pray for you, counsel and correct you if you are not ready to change it will be waste of time and other valuable resources. Because if you are not ready to change you will receive healing, counseling and encouragement but the moment you get out of their presence you will go back to your old habits.

3 Maintain what you have received

Everyone can receive good things but it is not everyone who can maintain what he or she has received. The secret of life is not in receiving but it lies in the issue of maintenance.

You can only maintain what you have received if

you keep good friends and reading materials that enriches your mind. You must fill your mind with positive thoughts. Wrong thoughts will come but you have been given authority over them i.e. you must reject them. Don't entertain them.

4. Destroy everything that might connect you to your old life. The final stage is to destroy everything

that can tempt or
connect you to your
old habits. If you have
marijuana in your
house you must
destroy it. If it is still in
your possession it
might act as a contact
point to draw you back
to your old life style.

If you have friends
who are not yet ready
to change, disconnect
yourself from those
relationships. You
should love those

friends at a distance
because the friends
we keep have great
influence in our lives.

In this world it is
better to be alone
rather to keep an
unhealthy relationship.
The problem is that we
like to say, do what
other people want so
that they can love or
appreciate us. Your life
comes first and others
people's lives follow
especially those who

are not ready to change.